MW00463407

The Porridge Manifesto: An amazing life starts with an amazing breakfast

ISBN-13: 978-1460981955
ISBN-10: 1460981952

Design: Alvaro Villanueva

Photography: Paige Green

The Porridge
MANIFESTO

An amazing life starts with an amazing breakfast

[signature: Rachel Cole]

by Rachel W Cole

CONTENTS

Introduction

While in graduate school, I worked the early shift at a local cafe — wake up time: 5:00 a.m. A slice of fruit galette or a warm scone suits me for a leisurely weekend morning nosh, but I require a breakfast of slightly more substance when I must stand, make semi-decent lattes and smile for eight hours.

In search of the perfect pre-dawn bite, I jotted down a list of my requirements.

- ☐ Quick and easy to prepare (or ready when I rise)
- ☐ Warm (to combat chilly morning air)
- ☐ Whole foods (to power me through)
- ☐ Delicious (because why eat anything that isn't?)

I recalled seeing an episode of Alton Brown's *Good Eats* — Oat Cuisine, to be exact — in which he slowly cooked steel cut oatmeal overnight. The idea of having a warm breakfast ready and waiting for me upon waking sounded heavenly and the fact that it would fuel me for the entire workday (or at least until my lunch break) made it even better.

As you'll see, for me Alton's oats sparked something much bigger and more exciting than simple oatmeal. Now, many years after my first bowl, porridge has become a part of my life. It's a way I care for myself and nourish others and a way to practice my own modern-day ritual.

In the following pages, I hope to inspire you — how you live and what you eat. I wish you endless, delicious bowls of porridge!

Rachel W. Cole
Oakland, California
February 2011

Special equipment

1.5 QUART SLOW COOKER

I know that you may be reluctant to acquire yet another kitchen appliance that would take up valuable countertop real estate or cupboard space. A small slow cooker, however, is crucial to making porridge — and because you'll use it all the time (I promise!) it's worth it.

I use a 1.5 quart Chefmate™ brand cooker. I bought it online, but they are also available in many local kitchen supply stores.

Some porridge converts I know use larger slow cookers to produce bigger batches and this may suit big families or those who prefer lots left over. If you take this route, get a model equipped with an automated shut-off feature, allowing you to choose the number of cooking hours before the cooker turns off. Whether you go with a small or large slow cooker, it is essential that your pot have multiple settings so the porridge can cook at low heat overnight.

I am frequently asked if a rice cooker will work. Having never tried one, I cannot say. If you can set a rice cooker on low heat and have it turn off after eight hours or so, then by all means give it a whirl. (And let me know!)

GLASS MASON JARS

There's nothing more inspiring than opening your kitchen cupboard to rows of mason jars filled with multi-hued, wholesome dry goods just waiting to be mixed, matched, and transformed into porridge. Glass jars simply have a tactile quality and classic aesthetic that outshines plastic bags or storage containers every time. (And glass poses no threat of a health risk as plastic may.)

If you don't currently keep (or hoard) your used glass jars as I do, you can start replacing plastics with a trip to the local hardware store or by taking in a few weekend yard sales. Once supplied with a set of glass jars, you may find your grocery store bulk aisle becomes for you a place of beauty. Have you ever stopped to really notice the delicate beauty of pink lentils or the glossy sheen on flax seeds? You'll know you're a convert when your jars creep out of the cupboard and take up homes in plain view.

BOWLS & SPOONS

I'm a bit of a porridge whisperer and try to let the ingredients "speak" to me when choosing what will go into my crock. Likewise when it comes time to eat I scan my collection of bowls and run my fingers over my spoons in search of the one that's just right for that morning. Treating yourself to the perfect bowl and spoon is one of the best parts of the porridge experience.

The day's favorite choices emerge in much the same way that the 'right' mug mysteriously makes itself known to tea or coffee drinkers. I've started to collect bowls that fit into my hand in very pleasing ways and have a certain depth and width that work for me. For spoons, I happen to like tiny demitasse or circular soup spoons. What's right for you is something only you can know.

I've included some of my favorite tool sources for porridge consumption in the Resources section.

Preparation

STORAGE & FRESHNESS

Whole grains, seeds, and nuts contain fat in their outer hull (the part removed in the refining process) and can spoil easily. Flax and hemp seeds in particular are likely to go rancid, especially if purchased as a pre-ground meal. These items should be bought in their freshest, whole state, stored in your fridge or freezer, and consumed soon after you bring them home. The best system I've discovered is to make four to six weeks' worth of porridge mix (i.e. your chosen dry ingredients, pre-combined), and keep it in a sealed storage container in a cold place. With this stash at hand, I don't need to run to the store frequently and can play with new variations whenever I want.

SELECTING INGREDIENTS FOR YOUR PORRIDGE

For starters, don't let the choices overwhelm you.

To make your mix, choose any combination of grains, legumes, nuts, and seeds (for suggestions, refer to my Incomplete Ingredient Lexicon at the end of this book) and just run with it. While there are certain ingredients that make regular appearances in my mix, no two batches of mine have been the same. I also don't bother with measuring exact quantities of anything.

Having eaten hundreds of bowls of porridge, I have learned through observation that ingredients react differently during the slow cooking process. Rolled oats, red lentils, and polenta, for example, become very soft and creamy, whereas whole-wheat berries, posole, adzuki beans, and quinoa largely keep their form. Neither of these outcomes is superior, and by mixing these two types of ingredients together I get a variety and contrast of textures that I enjoy.

In addition to exploring texture and flavor, you might also consider the nutrients and health components in each ingredient. That is, you can make an omega-3 mix (flax seeds, hemp seeds, topped with walnuts), or a sore-muscle, protein-rich mix (lentils, quinoa, whole grains, and nuts), or a gluten-free mix (polenta, millet, quinoa, brown rice, and amaranth). I don't mean to advocate for an eat-to-live mentality; I want simply to note that porridge is multi-dimensional.

Get a few batches under your belt and you'll find that making good porridge is a short journey of trial and error. You'll have the hang of it in no time. I strongly recommend beginning with a mix of just a few ingredients (three or four is a good start), and slowly adding others. That way, if you don't like something, you can easily identify it and banish it from your porridge repertoire

A final note on choosing what goes into your pot: you really will get out what you put in. If you use inexpensive, stale or low quality ingredients, your porridge likely will taste cheap, old and lackluster. Treating yourself to fresh, flavorful, high-quality foods can make all the difference in how much you enjoy your breakfast. If you're budget minded, you have no need to worry, as even the best porridge ingredients will cost less than the typical processed, packaged dry cereal. Many of the world's poorest people start their day with some version of porridge because, in addition to being nourishing and delicious, it's very economical.

(NOT) MEASURING

As I mentioned, I don't measure when I make porridge. This is a manifesto, not a cookbook. I've provided a starter recipe at the end, though, to get you going if you feel you need it.

One of the first things I learned soon after adopting my porridge habit was that I couldn't really make a single serving at a time because I needed to fill my mini crock sufficiently so the porridge would cook evenly and not burn. My basic method is to fill it 1/5 to 1/4 full (by eyesight) with my mix and cover that with water up to a half inch below the lip where the lid rests. You can and will change the ratio depending on how thin or thick you prefer your porridge.

Please note that you cannot use milk at this stage as the proteins in milk break down when heated for so long. (The cooker's user manual also advises against it.) Make your porridge with water, then, and when you eat it you can add milk — or any of the other "Lily-Gilders" in the Ingredient Lexicon.

FLIP THE SWITCH

Once you have your crock filled, set the dial to 'low' and leave it to do its work, letting your mix cook from six to ten hours. Some nights I put mix and water in the crock before dinner (especially if I'm going out for the evening) and then I just flip the 'on' dial right before I go to bed; other times I do the whole thing late at night. You'll figure out what works best for you and it will become second nature.

On occasions when I wake up early and want to go back to sleep, I just slip out of bed, turn the dial to "keep warm," and crawl back under the covers. After a long slumber, porridge makes a great brunch, lunch, or even dinner.

Enjoying

When my porridge is ready, I scoop out a cup or so into a bowl and allow the rest to cool in the crock, which I then cover and place in the fridge. That first morning, I enjoy it warm; on subsequent days (for as long as it lasts — usually four mornings) I like to have it cold. While I like it, others find cold porridge unpleasing. Try it both warm and cold to see what you think. If you like a little steam wafting from the bowl, you can easily reheat a serving or more gently on the stove, with a little milk or water.

Once I have my bowl of porridge ready, I put two types of goodies on top: the Crunchies and the Lily-Gilders. Some specific options for each of these are listed in the Incomplete Ingredient Lexicon.

How you choose to garnish yours is just part of the blissful creativity of making porridge. I encourage you to eat it slowly, savor it, and appreciate your unique creation; then be aware of how great your body feels from the first bite to the last, and throughout your day.

Ingredient musings

GRAINS

Grains come in various forms, from whole berries to cracked, rolled, flaked, or ground meal. A good rule of thumb is that the more processed the grain the less it will hold its shape when cooked.

Wheat has many names (especially if you include not-so-distant relatives, such as spelt and kamut) including bulgur (cracked wheat), farro, emmer, farina (Cream of Wheat), rolled wheat flakes, and of course, wheat berries.

Rice is the king (or queen) of porridge. More than half of the world's population eats rice two to three times each day, and it comes in infinite varieties (short grain, long grain, sweet, sticky, Bhutanese, etc.), I generally choose to use Massa Organics short-grain brown rice. I swear by this grain; it has the mysteriously exquisite combination of wonderful flavor and perfect texture.

Other great grains include rye, triticale (a hybrid of wheat and rye), millet, barley, quinoa, oats (don't use instant!), amaranth, teff and corn (posole, polenta, grits, frozen whole kernels).

You can also add bran (i.e. oat bran) or germ (i.e. wheat germ) if you want. These will boost the fiber and nutrient content, but aren't necessary if you are using whole ingredients. Also, you should know that both bran and germ can add to the 'mush' factor, which you may or may not want.

BEANS

For breakfast? Absolutely.

Beans provide delicious flavor, wonderful texture and, when combined with grains, a complete protein. However it's important to note that you're limited to quick cooking beans (i.e. lentils), fresh shelling beans (i.e. cranberry, fava, etc.), or dried beans that have been presoaked for at least 12 hours and, to be safe, par-cooked. Regular dried beans that have not been pre-soaked will not fully cook.

If you are concerned about an excessively "beany" flavor but want to try adding beans into your mix, start with red or yellow lentils, which have a mild flavor, lose their shape, and fade into the background. For a chunkier texture, try green (a.k.a du Puy) lentils, beluga lentils, whole mung beans, adzuki beans, fresh shelling beans (fava, cranberry, butter, etc.), and presoaked/par-cooked dried beans (garbanzo, pinto, black, etc.) that will hold at least partial shape overnight.

I am thrilled to see that America is experiencing a renewed appreciation for heirloom beans and I highly recommend seeking out some of these older varieties for your porridge, as well as for other cooking experiments

SEEDS

Most seeds do better as Crunchies (see the Ingredient Lexicon; Crunchies are to porridge as streusel is to cake) — except for flax, hemp, and chia seeds. These three, though, are better cooked overnight because they are hard to chew and digest when raw. Plus, flax and chia seeds impart a glutinous quality that makes your porridge nice and sticky-thick. But beware: because these two seeds serve as binding agents, too much could make your porridge excessively gluey. A light sprinkle of either goes a long way.

SPICES

Spices add a depth of flavor and new dimension to porridge. Add pumpkin pie spice mix to a batch that includes cubes of fresh pumpkins; add cinnamon to a batch with dried apples, or cardamom to a pot of basmati rice-based porridge along with a topping of mango and dried coconut.

DRIED FRUIT

Good quality fresh dried fruit becomes magical and plump when cooked overnight. Cheap dried fruit may become mushy and tasteless. If you aren't one for too much sugar in the morning, try this: add two chopped large dates, as they cook, the dates melt into the background and add a nice brown-sugar-like flavor. Other dried fruits that I frequently use are raisins, currants, prunes, and apricots.

VEGETABLES

I like nothing better than sweet ribbons of carrot or soft cubes of winter squash in my porridge pot. Obviously, these fresh ingredients do not go into the dry porridge mix I keep in my cupboard, but instead are added to the crock just before cooking. Any root vegetable will work — from parsnips to pumpkins. Unless I want a savory porridge, I stick to those with high sugar content, like beets, rather than turnips or baking potatoes. Cut firmer squash (peeled, if necessary) into small pieces so they will cook thoroughly.

TOPPINGS

Toppings make porridge — and porridge eaters — happy. Plain and simple. Toppings make porridge sing.

The Crunchies

These ingredients serve to add great texture — hence the name — and they can help add wonderful richness as well to your bowl. Most of these ingredients are higher in fat than the overnight ingredients and help to leave me feeling satisfied. Crunchies I turn to again and again include chopped walnuts, homemade granola, toasted coconut, and roasted pumpkin seeds.

The Lily-Gilders

These ingredients are just what the name suggests. Here are a few of my favorites (but note that I don't add all of these at the same time): a spoonful of almond butter, fresh blueberries, a drizzle of maple syrup, a swirl of raspberry jam, a pat of cultured butter, a dollop of crème fraiche, or shavings of chocolate.

Most of the Lily-Gilders are the cherry to your porridge sundae, but you need your hot fudge sauce too. To discover which liquid and how much is right for you, I like to examine cereal preferences. Generally, I think that cereal people can be divided into two categories:

TEAM MILK: Those who love cold, refreshing milk as much as, or more than, they do crunchy flakes or wheaty biscuits. This group is generous with their pour and are known for finishing off the bowl by bringing it up to their mouths for one last slurp.

TEAM CEREAL: Those who pour as little milk as possible and don't think twice about pouring any extra down the drain (even if it is chocolate flavored).

Regardless of which group you fall into (I'm Team Milk, all the way), adding a little or a lot of liquid love can be great thing. Here are a few of my favorite wet additions: whole farm-fresh milk, coconut milk, fresh almond milk, and whole-milk plain yogurt.

Savory

If you're thinking of going the savory route, consider making your porridge with chicken stock or vegetable broth. Once it's ready, topping options include: miso, soy sauce, caramelized onions, sautéed vegetables, grated sharp cheese, or a finishing spice like dukkah or zataar.

8 reasons porridge will rock your day & your life

1. Nature intended us to eat WHOLE foods. Porridge is made up of whole foods. If you ask me, nature intended for us to eat porridge.

2. Michael Pollan says "Eat Food. Not too much. Mostly Plants." Porridge is food. Porridge is hard to OD on. Porridge vittles come straight from the plant kingdom.

3. With porridge, you'll have no need for 'second breakfast'. You'll stay full till lunch.

4. Carbs (at least the unrefined kind) are good, good for you, and tasty. Porridge is carb-o-rific.

5. Nothing tastes as good as homemade. Porridge is homemade (unless you make it somewhere else).

6. Wanna eat local and organic? Just put local and organic stuff in your porridge. Done and done.

7. You won't want to hit the snooze button. Hello sunshine!

8. Pleasure is a food group (if you ask me) and before 10:00 a.m. you'll be on your way to getting all your daily servings of this oft-neglected nutrient.

My incomplete
ingredient lexicon

Consider this a shopping list, a to-do list, and an inspiration list... and by all means, add your own ideas.

THE MIX

adzuki beans

amaranth

chia seeds

corn (posole/hominy, polenta/cornmeal/grits, whole frozen kernels)

dried fruit

flax seeds

kamut, spelt, farro

lentils (red, yellow, split, du Puy, beluga)

oats (groats, steel cut, rolled)

quinoa

rice (brown, Bhutanese, forbidden black, wild, etc.)

sweet root vegetables

triticale flakes

wheat (berries, bulgur, rolled)

THE CRUNCHIES

almonds, walnuts, pecans

homemade granola

pumpkin seeds (a.k.a. pepitas)

sunflower seeds, sesame seeds, poppy seeds

toasted coconut

THE LILY-GILDERS

brown sugar, palm sugar, muscovado sugar

butter

buttermilk, yogurt

chocolate chips or shavings

crème fraiche

crystallized ginger

fresh seasonal fruit

fruit jam, jelly, marmalade

honey, maple syrup, agave syrup, molasses

lemon curd

mascarpone

milk, cream

nut butter (peanut, almond, etc.)

soy milk, almond milk, coconut milk

yogurt, kefir

SAVORY TOPPERS

(Note: you can cook savory porridge using stock or broth)

a poached or fried egg

caramelized onions or roasted vegetables

fermented goodies: kim chi or sauerkraut

fresh herbs: basil, chives, cilantro, etc.

mild cheeses: cottage cheese, ricotta, fromage blanc

miso, soy sauce, nori, gomasio, toasted sesame oil, scallions

nut or seed oils: walnut, hazelnut, pumpkin seed

salsa and/or guacamole

sharp cheeses: cheddar, gouda, etc.

spices: dukkah or zaatar

Resources

Most large grocery stores carry a range of whole grains, dried beans, and other natural foods. Alternatively, health food stores are a reliable source for these ingredients, often selling a wide variety in bulk. In case you have trouble finding what you are looking for or if you just want to get yourself to a few of my favorite porridge treats and tools, I've listed mail-order sources here:

HEIRLOOM GRAINS, BEANS, & SEEDS

Anson Mills
> *www.ansonmills.com*

Blue Bird Grain Farms
> *www.bluebirdgrainfarms.com*

Massa Organics
> *www.massaorganics.com*

Native Seed Search
> *www.nativeseeds.org*

Rancho Gordo
> *www.ranchogordo.com*

HANDCRAFTED SPICE BLENDS

Juliet Mae Spices
www.julietmae.com

JAMS & MARMALADE

Blue Chair Fruit
www.bluechairfruit.com

BOWLS & SPOONS

Goodwill, Thrift Stores, Yard Sales, Flea Markets
Many of my favorite kitchen tools were discovered at a second-hand store and cost less than ten cents. I highly recommend an afternoon spent sorting through bins of used silverware; there are often real gems to be found.

Heath Ceramics
Top-notch stunning tableware for those who can afford it.
www.heathceramics.com

Hausmittel
Some very stylish vintage mavens run this sweet Etsy shop filled with rediscovered kitchen treasures.
www.etsy.com/shop/hausmittel

Pigeon Toe Ceramics

> I treated myself to a bowl from this Portland-based ceramicist. It is still my favorite porridge bowl, bar none.
> *www.pigeontoeceramics.com*

A PORRIDGE EATER'S COMPANION COOKBOOK COMPENDIUM

DIY Delicious by Vanessa Barrington (Chronicle, 2010)

Feeding the Whole Family by Cynthia Lair (Sasquatch Books, 2008)

Good to the Grain by Kim Boyce (Stewart, Tabori & Chang, 2010)

How to Cook Everything Vegetarian by Mark Bittman (Wiley, 2007)

Super Natural Cooking by Heidi Swanson (Ten Speed, 2007)

Vegetarian Cooking for Everyone by Deborah Madison (Clarkson Potter, 2007)

Whole Grains by Lorna Sass (Clarkson Potter, 2006)

Wholefood by Jude Blereau (Running Press, 2007)

The porridge recipe 1.0

This recipe works for a 1.5-quart slow cooker. If you are using a different size, adjust accordingly.

THE MIX

½ cup short grain brown rice

¼ cup amaranth

¼ cup steel-cut oats

¼ cup posole

¼ cup pink lentils

¼ cup quinoa

1 t flax or chia seeds

1 t ground cinnamon

2 medjool dates, pitted and chopped

THE CRUNCHIES

homemade granola

THE LILY-GILDERS

maple syrup

fresh seasonal fruit

whole milk yogurt

Follow steps outlined in Preparation on page 12.

About Rachel

I guide people towards pleasure-filled, nourishing, self-designed lives. And I do it through inspiring coaching and creative collaborations. I have life coaching superpowers thanks to The Coaches Training Institute, a Masters degree in Holistic Health Education from John F. Kennedy University, and a glorious gap between my front teeth. I'm on a mission to trigger courageous creative living and put porridge on more people's breakfast tables. I want to know: what are you *truly* hungry for?

You can find me at www.rachelwcole.com or my kitchen table in Oakland, California.

Made in the USA
Charleston, SC
16 November 2011